Capital Resources and the Economy

Jennifer Overend Prior, Ph.D.

Consultant

Caryn Williams, M.S.Ed.
Madison County Schools
Huntsville, AL

Image Credits: Cover & pp.1, 29 (top) Blend Images/ Alamy; p.26 Cornelius Kalk/age fotostock; p.27 Jeff Greenough/age fotostock; p.9 (top) David Price/Alamy; p.6 (left) Mary Evans Picture Library/Alamy; p.17 (middle) Michael Neelon/Alamy; pp.2–3 Myrleen Pearson/Alamy; p.15 (top) Rawdon Wyatt/Alamy; p.15 (background) Richard Levine/Alamy; p.16 Hulton-Deutsch Collection/ Corbis; p.25 (top) Alistair Berg/Getty Images; p.19 (top) Richard Drury/Getty Images; p.14 The Granger Collection, NYC/The Granger Collection; pp.3, 10 (bottom), 13 (top), 17 (top), 23 (top), 28 (top), 21 iStock; p.10 (left) Bourne & Shepherd/National Geographic Creative; pp.12–13 Attila Balazs/EPA/Newscom; p.8 (top) Rolf Schultes/Newscom; pp.6 (right), 7 Wikimedia Commons; all other images from Shutterstock.

Library of Congress Cataloging-in-Publication Data

Prior, Jennifer Overend, 1963-
  Capital resources and the economy / Jennifer Overend Prior, Ph.D.
    pges cm
  Audience: K to Grade 3.
  Includes index.
  ISBN 978-1-4333-7372-5 (pbk.)
  SBN 978-1-4807-5158-3 (ebook)
  1. Capital—Juvenile literature.
  2. Infrastructure (Economics)—Juvenile literature. I. Title.
  HC79.C3P697 2014
  332´.041—dc23
                                        2014010588

Teacher Created Materials
5301 Oceanus Drive
Huntington Beach, CA 92649-1030
http://www.tcmpub.com
ISBN 978-1-4333-7372-5

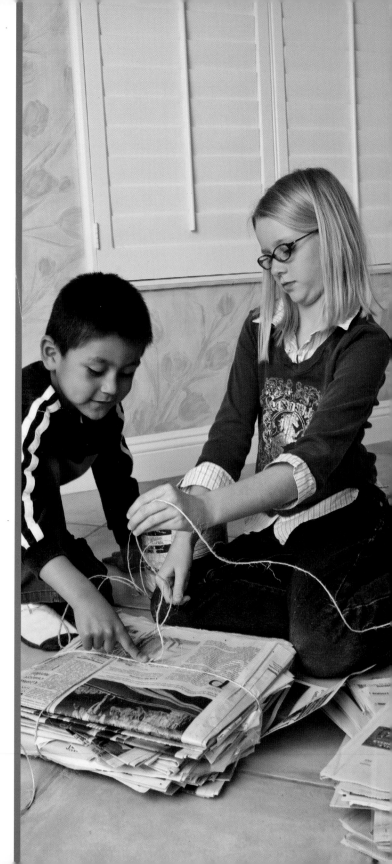

Table of Contents

Water is a natural resource.

What Are Capital Resources?

We have many **resources** (REE-sawr-suhz) available to us. A resource is something that we can use. Some of them are **natural resources**. This means that they are found in nature. Water and trees are natural resources. We drink water and use it for many things. We use trees to make houses and paper.

A hammer is a capital resource.

Capital resources are things that people use to make goods and provide services. For example, wood is a natural resource. People can use wood to make a house. But nails are capital resources. People use nails to hold the wood together. We could not build a house without capital resources.

Think about some of the things around you right now. What tools do you think were needed to make your chair? What was used to turn trees into pencils? All of these things are capital resources.

Capital Resources Then and Now

People have always used capital resources. Our **ancient** (EYN-shuhnt) **ancestors** used them. When we dig in the ground where the first humans lived, we find tools. Our ancestors used these tools to hunt animals. These tools were capital resources.

Ancient Resources

Our ancestors made fishhooks, nets, spears, arrowheads, and many other tools to help them hunt and fish.

Our ancestors turned rocks into tools such as arrowheads.

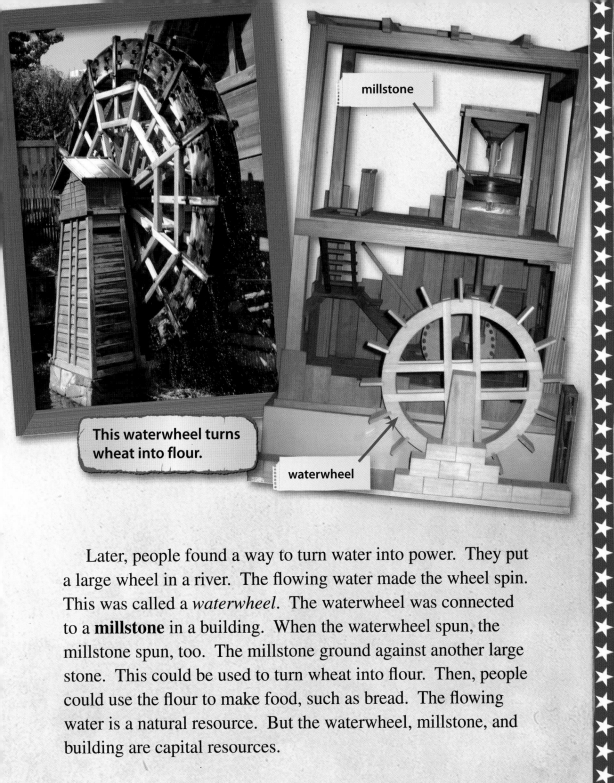

millstone

waterwheel

This waterwheel turns wheat into flour.

Later, people found a way to turn water into power. They put a large wheel in a river. The flowing water made the wheel spin. This was called a *waterwheel*. The waterwheel was connected to a **millstone** in a building. When the waterwheel spun, the millstone spun, too. The millstone ground against another large stone. This could be used to turn wheat into flour. Then, people could use the flour to make food, such as bread. The flowing water is a natural resource. But the waterwheel, millstone, and building are capital resources.

We use many different capital resources today. Much of the food we eat comes from nature. Eggs are a natural resource. Chickens lay them on farms. Then, the eggs are brought to stores where people buy them. But most of us do not like to eat raw, or uncooked, eggs. We need to use capital resources before we eat them. The trucks that take the eggs from the farm to the store are capital resources. The frying pans we use to cook the eggs are capital resources, too.

This farmer collects eggs to be brought to stores.

Think about the bricks used to make buildings. Bricks are made of a mixture of natural resources, such as sand, clay, and water. But people need capital resources to make bricks, too. We need tools to shape the bricks and ovens to heat them. All of these items are capital resources. Capital resources help us use natural resources in different ways.

This man uses capital resources to make bricks.

People have always used capital resources to make their lives simpler. In the past, people used tools such as baskets to make gathering food easier. But back then, people had to live close to sources of food and water. Today, food and water can be brought to us.

Long ago, people had to get water from a river or a well. Wells are holes deep in the ground with water at the bottom. Today, houses have plumbing. This is a system of pipes that brings water inside. People use this water for drinking, cooking, and taking baths.

well

This woman uses a basket to collect berries.

basket

Unlike our ancestors, we do not have to hunt and gather food. Instead, we have markets. Food is grown on farms. The farms can be miles away. They can even be in other countries! The food is then boxed and shipped to our markets. Using capital resources has made our lives much easier.

Shopping in markets lets us choose many different kinds of food to eat.

This worker uses capital resources to make Legos®.

Goods and Services

Did you know that you use goods every day? Goods are things that people buy and sell. Have you ever bought a toy or a video game? These are goods. People use capital resources to make them. They use machines to make most toys. Computers are needed to make video games. Machines and computers are capital resources.

Producers and Consumers

When people make goods or provide services, they are called *producers*. When people use goods and services, they are called *consumers*. You are a producer when you do chores around the house. You are a consumer when you buy a toy. We are all producers and consumers.

This man uses capital resources to provide a service.

We also use many kinds of services. A service is something that a person does for you. Have you ever eaten at a restaurant? The cooks who make the food are providing a service. So are the people who bring you the food. The items used to make the food, such as ovens and pots, are capital resources. The tray the server uses to bring the food to your table is a capital resource, too. People use capital resources to provide their services.

The Economy

You may have heard about the **economy** (ih-KON-uh-mee). This is the system in which people use money to buy goods and services. Capital resources are a part of this system.

People use capital resources to make money. An artist may spend money to buy a paintbrush. The artist uses the paintbrush to paint a picture. The picture is sold to a buyer. The artist used a capital resource to make money. The paintbrush is the capital resource. The artist can now use that money to buy more goods or services. This keeps the economy going.

Sometimes the economy is strong. This means that most people have jobs. They are making money and spending it on goods and services. This is called a *boom period*. Other times, the economy is weak. This is when a lot of people do not have jobs. They are not making money, so they cannot buy goods and services. This is called a *bust period*.

These people wait outside a government office to try to find work during a bust period in 1931.

An artist sells his paintings.

People have money to spend on goods and services during a boom period.

Supply and **demand** are key parts of an economy. Supply is how much of something there is to buy or use. Demand is how many people want to buy or use that thing.

Supply and demand are always changing. Sometimes, there is a lot of demand for something. This means that many people want to buy it at the same time. Lots of people want soup on a rainy day. When people buy a lot of soup, there may not be any left later in the day. Demand is high and supply is low.

But other times, there is very little demand for that same thing. Very few people want soup on a hot, sunny day. This means that there will probably be lots of soup left at the end of the day. Demand is low and supply is high.

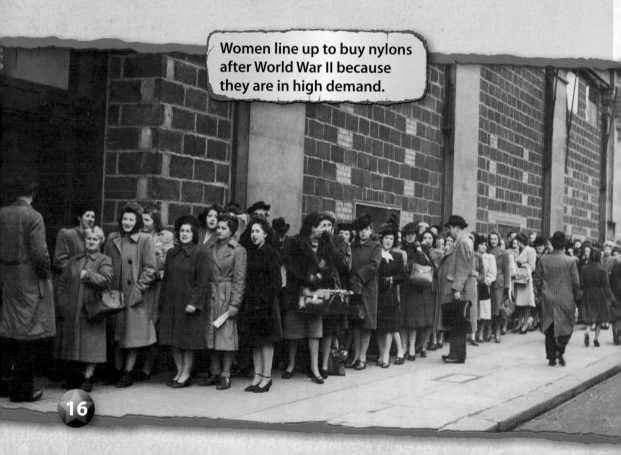

Women line up to buy nylons after World War II because they are in high demand.

Sometimes, things go on sale when there is a low demand.

These people wait in line to buy new electronics which are in high demand.

In some countries, the government sets the prices for goods and services. This is called a *command economy*. This is because leaders command, or tell, people what prices to set. They do this to make sure prices are never too high or too low.

In the United States, we have a free market economy. This means that the government does not control the prices of goods and services. Instead, people set the prices for things they sell. In a free market economy, prices are decided based on supply and demand.

Here is an example. The owner of a store can sell gum for any price she wants. She can set the price high when there is low demand. But she will not sell much gum. She can set the price low when there is high demand. People will buy the gum quickly, but she would have made more money if she had set the price high. Prices are always changing in a free market economy.

Human Resources

There are natural resources and capital resources. But there is another resource—people! We need people to grow food and to build houses. People work in stores and in schools. They make goods and perform services that we need. They are called **human resources**.

We would not have capital resources without human resources. To build a house you need natural resources, such as wood. You also need capital resources, such as a hammer and nails. But these things are not useful if there are no people. It is the people that use the tools to build the house. Those people are human resources.

human resource

natural resource

capital resource

You are a human resource, too! Have you ever helped make dinner? You may need some natural resources, such as water and eggs. And you will probably need some capital resources, such as a stove and pan. But the meal cannot be made unless you help make it. You are the human resource. You turn the resources into dinner.

This machine pulls oil up from under the ground.

Using Our Resources Carefully

Long ago, people only used a small amount of Earth's natural resources. They used water for drinking, cleaning, and farming. They used a few trees to build their houses.

Today, we use more natural resources than ever before. We cut down large forests to build more houses. We dig deep in the ground to find oil. These natural resources help us build big cities. They help power our cars and homes.

These logs were cut from trees in a rainforest.

Some of the natural resources we use, such as water, keep coming back. We can collect more water when it rains. These are called *renewable* (ri-NOO-uh-buhl) *resources*. Of course, we still have to be careful not to use too much so that there is always enough. But other natural resources, such as oil, do not come back. There is a set amount of oil in the world. These are called *nonrenewable resources*.

Our capital resources can make many things. But, we can only make these things if there are enough natural resources left. We need to be careful about how we use the world's resources.

Some resources we need are **scarce**. That means they are rare. There are not a lot of them. This can affect the way we live. In some countries, food is scarce. People do not always have enough to eat. If oil is scarce, people will not have gas to drive their cars.

When resources are scarce, we need to change how we live. It is important for us to **conserve** resources so that we have them when we need them. To conserve means to use something carefully. We can conserve **electricity** by turning off lights when people are not in a room. If we waste the resources we have, we will use them all up.

Turning off lights and using dimmers help conserve resources.

One way to conserve is to **recycle**. Recycling is turning used things into new things that can be used again. People recycle things such as plastic bottles, glass jars, and paper. By recycling, people can use the same natural resources again and again.

Recycling is a great way to conserve Earth's resources.

Earth Day

Every April 22, the United States and over 100 other countries celebrate Earth Day. On this day, people wear green and do things to help the environment (en-VAHY-ruhn-muhnt). This day helps to remind us that we need to conserve Earth's natural resources.

A World of Resources

People around the world are connected through resources. All countries use capital resources. They use them to make things from natural resources. Every country has different natural resources. Countries often buy and sell goods with one another. This lets them get all the things that they want and need.

This worker is a human resource.

Natural, human, and capital resources were used to make this game.

Think about resources the next time that you play a game. Think about all the resources it took to make it. Does the game have plastic parts? Plastic is made from natural resources. Think of the human resources. People had to design the game. Then, think about all the capital resources. Are there screws holding the game together? Did a machine build it? Was a paintbrush used to paint it? Capital resources can help turn natural resources into many things. They make things that we use and enjoy every day.

List It!

Think of a good you would like to make for your family or friends. Maybe you would like to bake cookies for your neighbors. Or maybe you would like to paint a picture to share with your family. Make a list of all the capital resources you will need to make that good. Then, make your good to share with your family or friends.

This girl lists the capital resources she will need.

This boy makes cookies with his dad.

Glossary

ancestors—the people who lived before us

ancient—relating to a period of time long ago in the past

capital resources—things that people use to make goods and provide services

conserve—to use carefully

demand—the amount of people who want goods or services

economy—the system by which goods and services are made, bought, and sold

electricity—a form of energy that is carried through wires and is used to operate lights and machines

human resources—people with skills who are able to do work

millstone—one of two large, round stones used for grinding grain in a mill

natural resources—things existing in the natural world that a country can use

recycle—to make something new from something that has been used before

resources—things that a country has and can use to make money

scarce—a very small amount or number

supply—the amount of goods or services that are offered for sale

Index

Your Turn!

Object Challenge

Choose an object from your classroom. What natural resources were needed to make the object? What capital resources were needed to make it? What human resources were needed to make it? Make a chart and list the resources that might have been needed.